CELEBRATE YOUR EXISTENCE

"Celebration is appreciating the possibilities hidden in the folds of life even while being aware of all the evil and frustration that is there. . . . Celebration is delight in the elemental simplicities—the deed well done, the thought well spoken, the beauty freshly seen, the relation of intimacy, the imagination inventing new dreams."

—From *On Becoming Human* by Ross Snyder. Copyright © 1967 by Abingdon Press.

CELEBRATE YOUR EXISTENCE

By Lucille Oliver

Preliminary design by Clarice Ward

Copyright © 1971

HERALD PUBLISHING HOUSE

Independence, Missouri

Library of Congress Catalog Card No. 79-147022
ISBN-0-8309-0042-X

Printed in the United States of America

CONTENTS

PROLOGUE

The last few years have had a tremendous impact on my thinking. Reared in the traditional Christian faith and being optimistic by nature, I have found that my religion has always sustained me. I try to be a positive person. However, after passing the forty-year milestone, I sometimes have felt that life has been going downhill in many respects—not the least being my inability to comprehend what has been happening in the world, especially with the response of youth. I discovered that so-called traditional religion failed to produce the desired results. Peace and brotherhood seemed as far away as ever, an impossible dream which would remain just that.

My husband, a high priest appointee-minister for the Reorganized Church of Jesus Christ of Latter Day Saints, and I have tried very hard for the past twenty years to assist others in bringing the kingdom of God to the earth. Sometimes I have felt it was twenty years wasted.

Six years ago I reentered the labor market as an administrative assistant in the Department of Medical Research at Blodgett Hospital in Grand Rapids, Michigan. Because of my association there with Dr. Vernon E. Wendt, cardiologist and director of the department, and many others in the hospital, my mind began expanding as I encountered the fascinating world of research and assisted in a small way with man's efforts to sustain life.

After three years there, following a change in directorship, I accepted a challenging position on the staff of the local YWCA. This largest women's organization in the world is undergoing rapid change as it seeks to become relevant to the world of today and fulfill its responsibility in barrier-breaking programs promoting peace and dignity for all men. I have met many people of various races and creeds, and I have witnessed a hopelessness in people as they struggle to meet the multitudinous problems of this age. I sense a dire need for human beings to recapture a hope in the new tomorrow, a vision that will sustain them, and an energy that will enable them to endure today while building that tomorrow.

In this process I have rediscovered the thrill of knowing that the kingdom of peace is being built on the earth. Amid the turmoil and agony I can see the plan of God coming to fruition as men seek to understand themselves and to relate to their fellows. I desire to share this miracle with you. This little book has been written with the sincere wish that it may help you celebrate your existence as I have learned to do. I am indebted to Ross Snyder for his book, *On Becoming Human,* which helped me with my celebration. And there are others who have made a unique contribution to my search:

- Katie, my dear friend in Uganda, with whom I shared deep convictions about peace and love
- Nettie, Evelyn, Faye, Mary Lu, and Julia who helped me understand and respect the black community
- Nan and all those under thirty who helped me feel "in" by selecting me as their poet laureate at the YWCA training in Chicago, 1968
- The "Group" of Grand Rapids, who are attempting to build the kingdom in a fantastic way
- Cliff and Clarice who gave much needed encouragement
- Fran and Ted who are so good to everyone and who have learned much about celebration
- Arliss and Sharon who never fail to let me know they care
- Margo who always sees the beautiful

- Little Vern, age two, who allowed me to see deep into the soul of a child
- Mildred and Earl, whose friendship has survived time, distance, and age
- My own siblings, Bob, Carol, and John, whom I love very much and who helped me grow in awareness
- My grandchildren—Patty, Anita, Tonie, Robin, Robert, Jr., and York—who keep me young
- Sister Rose from Guyana, South America, a groovy nun who loved to celebrate
- My loving husband, Lee, with whom I have challenged life for over thirty years
- And all who have assisted me celebrate my existence. To them I joyfully dedicate this book. My prayer is that it may bring a conviction of hope and that all who read will find delight in being . . . especially women.

L. O.

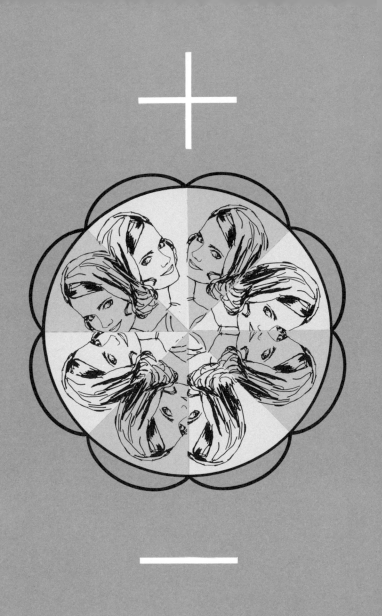

Chapter I

KALEIDOSCOPE

"Celebration means nevertheless, Come hell or high water I still live in grace and generosity, in reverence and appreciation appropriating the life possible in my moment of existence."—Ross Snyder

Are you happy being a woman? Have you ever looked objectively at the kaleidoscope of life? Can you see how the bits and pieces of joy, wonder, unhappiness, and despair blend together in a maze of human energy? Ever wonder why you're here, where you're going, what makes you tick? You must be aware that a woman's life today is very different from that of her grandmother or even her mother. It is an amazing age—probably the most challenging era women have ever known, for they now have the ability and opportunity to play the most important role that ever has been offered them.

For centuries women were considered less than

first-class citizens. They had to satisfy man's erotic desire, bear his children, and be the keepers of his house. Females were considered the weaker sex. They did not discuss politics or business. They were not to use their brains except when it pertained to rearing children and keeping house.

With the beginning of the industrial revolution, women in the United States began asserting their cravings to become whole persons. Though the men thought the day would never come, women finally did secure the right to vote.

Today women are being liberated in a revolution of their own. A sign in a Michigan YWCA shouted in bold, black letters, "WOMEN CAN THINK AS WELL AS TYPE." One man who read the sign told the executive, "When you find one like that, send her over."

Actually the revolution began in the 1920's. Today we are confronted with the result of this turning point. We are experiencing further agonizing as we are tossed amid the morass of sexuality's various shades and meanings thrown to us from many directions. Sex is a very important part of our makeup. Today we are being forced to take another look at this side of our nature.

As women we play many roles during our lifetimes. An infant literally bursts from the mother's womb into a noisy, dirty, fragmented world. If it is fortunate it will be surrounded by love and devotion. Its needs will be adequately met, and it will mature. Educators say that by the time a child is three years old its personality and basic character traits are formed. Paul Goodman's *Growing Up Absurd* describes society as an "apparently closed room in which there is a large rat race as the dominant center of attention." It is very hard to grow up in this condition, Goodman says, for there is no true sense of community that might sustain, inspire, and nurture young people until they can act on their own with fully developed powers. Sometimes the infant develops into an insecure, fearful, frustrated person who cannot adjust to the "slings and arrows of outrageous fortune" and in turn begets others who follow the same pattern.

Before we have discovered who we are and why, we are thrown into society as wife and mother—the traditional role of woman. Here the demands are quite keen. Often we go unprepared into this part of our lives. We have not matured. As a result the divorce rate is higher today than it has ever been in our history. I believe marriage was intended to be a mutual path along which two people walk sharing burdens and delights. Too often one or the other demands total allegiance while refusing to reciprocate.

Children are caught in this web and never allowed their own maturity. They must be given independence from parents in order to become human beings in their own right. Many adults have never been allowed this freedom so necessary to the establishment of a successful home. The home is still the basic unit of society, contrary to what many are saying, but the environment within that home is undergoing tremendous changes.

The rearing of children combines tensions brought on by demands of both husband and family. Today over 41 percent of American women work outside the home. This contributes to the stress of everyday living. Three of today's great killers are the phone with its interruptions, the clock with its appointments, and the calendar with its apprehension. These are the things that keep people jumping and jumpy, causing stress and strain and preventing their being fully human.

Dr. Hans Selye of Montreal believes that the cause of nearly all disease may turn out to be a chemical imbalance in the body caused by such stress. If this proves to be correct, it could be one of the most significant medical advances of this century. The housewife tries to run her home, bring up boisterous children, be charming and sexy for her mate, be active in the PTA and the church, and engage in civic and community work. *If there is time,* she can try to fulfill her own identity needs. This hectic schedule is often accompanied by excess worry and frustration brought on by her failure to know who she is and why she is here.

Chemical imbalance in the body is governed mainly by three tiny glands—the pituitary which nestles under the brain and the two adrenals which sit astride the kidneys. Their principal job is to adapt the body to all kinds of stress. When people go at the pace just described, these glands attempt to compensate by pouring hormones into the blood to relieve the stress. For a time they succeed. They get tired, chemical imbalance occurs and the system breaks down. Although some people may work better for a time under such pressure, everyone has a stress tolerance, and when this breaking point is reached, illness—physical, mental, or both—results (see chapter on stress).

Some women can take more of life's darts than others. Some react to every situation, while a few are able to act in a counter-move. No two human beings respond exactly alike. Two women lose their husbands through sudden death. One gives up, goes into a decline, accepts self-pity, and becomes morbid. Without purpose or goal, the family disintegrates and her children grow up the best way they can. The other knows the extreme sadness of her loss but keeps her balance, holds her home together, meets the responsibilities and obligations of each day. What is the difference? What is the plus factor that causes one to grow under trials and another to fold up completely? Is it physical stamina, spiritual stability, financial security? No one can be sure, but it's certain that the woman who understands life can accept any limitation and carry on to the best of her ability with fidelity.

A prominent woman who has shown great courage and determination is Rose Kennedy. She has known extreme sorrow and loss in her life. Four of her children have met violent deaths. Two were killed in airplane crashes, and two were cut down by the assassin's bullets. One of her daughters is mentally retarded and has spent her life in an institution. Her husband was stricken and lay for years without being able to function or even to speak. Yet Rose Kennedy, at eighty, is still able to play nine holes of golf and is a very dynamic woman who has not allowed the heartaches of life to defeat her. She taught her children to walk bravely into life, without allowing fear to overcome them. Joe, the oldest son, volunteered to fly the explosive-loaded plane which resulted in his death. John, the President, refused to separate himself from the people with a bullet-proof bubble top on his car. Bobby, the senator, mingled with the crowds he sought to influence, never thinking of his own safety, which resulted in the tragedy of his death. Because they did not fear death, they were able to live life.

Dr. Viktor Frankl, who spent years in the concentration camps in Germany and survived, reminds us that suffering has a supreme purpose in life if we can accept the responsibility for that suffering and turn it into meaning.

It isn't so much what happens to us as what we do with what happens that adds up to whether or not we can celebrate our existence—which is what life's all about. There is joy in sorrow. How can we recognize the sweet unless we also taste the bitter? In the frantic pace most of us keep today, there is increasing need to celebrate and respond to being fully human.

One young mother said to me, "I'm getting so accustomed to being tense that when I'm calm I get nervous." Mothers do have a difficult time meeting all of life's demands. There is so much to know concerning children—the first child especially. A mother of four confessed, "When I had my first baby, I phoned the doctor every time he sneezed. Today my youngest swallowed a nickel. I looked at him and said, 'Young man, that money comes out of your allowance.' "

Can one learn the true meaning of life while there is still time to apply it?

Vital to such understanding is developing a self-image which acknowledges purpose in all life. It is to be aware of the demons which plague us from time to time. We all have such demons, and if we would examine closely the psychological reactions which are interfering with the normalcy of behavior in a neurotic, we would be compelled to recognize that they are no different than our own, merely more intense; they are still fear, jealousy, susceptibility, anger, dissimulation, self-pity, sentimentality, erotic desire, and depression.

Psychologists recognize four principal troublemakers in this realm of the personal unconscious: fear, guilt, inferiority feelings, and hate. Recognizing these demons and bringing them out into the open is the first step to developing a healthy self-image. Jesus told his followers, "The kingdom of heaven is within you." Then what about the kingdom of hell? The woman who harbors fear, hate, guilt, and inferiority feelings has within her the kingdom of hell.

Fear drains the body of needed energy, and one cannot find the true joy in life with such fears prevalent. They must be overcome by faith. Recognition of such fears is the beginning of self-honesty. No one knowingly chooses to house these demons, but ignorance of the laws governing the internal world is not a sufficient excuse. Both kingdoms lie within every woman. She alone can choose to unlock one or the other, to dwell in harmony or to live in chaos.

Some women are so fearful they project disaster far in advance. There is no need to cross bridges before we get to them. Actually, we can't cross any sooner, and attempts to do so merely add additional burdens of stress which become unbearable.

One of our predominant fears is that of growing old. We do not believe the poet when he said, "Come grow old along with me; the best of life is yet to be—the last for which the first was made." Why do we hate to grow old? Is it because we are afraid of being useless? The dilemma of today is not in being useless but in deciding where to help first. We can become involved in other people and their problems. Volunteer work is needed desperately in every area of life. In order to do this successfully, however, we must satisfy our own ego. We need to grow to be mature people who respond, who are aware, and who love even those who do not love us. The feelings of worthlessness are not products of old age but represent development of emotional patterns established earlier in life. We can remain young by living in the present; by becoming involved in life; and by having faith in

God, in ourselves, and in our fellowmen. There must be time in our daily lives for contemplation and meditation, a place where we can "be still and know."

In the following chapters I hope to present some insight into the paradox that is each of us—who we are, why we're here, and where we're going. Nothing is more deadly to the human spirit than dull, aimless, day-to-day wandering without goal or purpose. Human energies are never more wasted than when spent in frantic busyness devoid of meaning.

We are travelers together on the spaceship earth. We need to band with each other in mutual endeavors. We can learn how to contribute to each other in the process of becoming fully human, realizing we are a part of a vast, perfectly created universe. To re-create this unity is our goal, and to celebrate our existence is one step toward reaching that perfection.

> *Within your life world you are meant to be a center of aliveness. . . . You are a center of decision and fidelity over a period of time.*
>
> —*Ross Snyder*

Chapter II

MIRROR, MIRROR ON THE WALL

This story is told about the German philosopher Schopenhauer. Considerably disheveled in appearance, he was sitting on a park bench in Frankfurt when the park attendant, thinking the untidy stranger to be a tramp, approached him with the query, "Who are you?" He replied sadly, "I wish I knew."

Children often ask the question, "Mamma, why was I born?" Four hundred years ago the English dramatist-poet William Shakespeare placed on the lips of Macbeth this comment: "Life's but a walking shadow, a poor player, that struts and frets his hour upon the stage and then is heard no more; it is a tale told by an idiot, full of sound and fury, signifying nothing."

Why were you born? Do you believe that life is an accident or a planned event? Is life meant to be a tale told by an idiot? Do you think that this world is an iceberg or a ship? Does it have direction, or does it float aimlessly through time and space?

In the well-known fairy tale the queen stood before her magic mirror each morning. "Mirror, mirror on the wall," she would chant, "who is the fairest of them all?" Quite assured of the answer, she would vainly await the reply, "Thou, O queen, art the fairest in all the land." One morning, however, the answer was different. In wrath the queen heard that another was fairer than she. Her ego was wounded and from that moment she spent her life trying to find and kill her rival.

What is the image you have of yourself? What does your magic mirror tell you? What about that subconscious looking glass within the nine tenths of your mind that can be either monster or healer? Are you aware that hidden within is an image which controls your thoughts and actions? Self-image is formed early in childhood. This constantly changes as you react to situations in life. If you always react—never act—in any given situation, if you become an echo rather than a voice, your self-image will be one that causes grave trouble, and often you will feel as one put it, "Life is a bad joke that isn't even funny."

It is extremely important that we place the emphasis on the plus factors in our personalities. To do this we need to know ourselves, face our limitations, honor them, and realize that we have other attributes more valuable than the physical image we see in a mirror. We need to be reminded today that we are spiritual beings, that inner space is more important than outer space. The ability to form sincere, enduring friendships depends on the strength of our self-image.

Some would have us believe that we were created in the image of monkeys. I confess that many act as if this were the case. I prefer, however, to believe that we were created in the image of God with a divine spark within which can motivate us to love our fellows and to live at peace with them. This is the only thing that gives meaning to my life and to the lives of those around me. I do not propose to argue evolution. I believe man did evolve, but within his own species and not from apes or fish.

We project an image of some kind to ourselves, our families, and those around us. Is it real? We can fool ourselves and others a good deal of the time, but we can never fool God. He knows our hearts and sees deep within the secret places where we won't even allow ourselves to enter.

In order to have a healthy self-image, we must have respect for self. The word "respect" means "to look at"—the ability to see things as they really are.

From childhood, adolescence, and maturity to middle and old age each woman meets life in terms of her own inner evaluation of herself—her concept of herself as a woman. This yardstick may be telescoped or elongated by her emotional status and intellectual capacity or compromised by the comparisons she draws between herself, her mother or sisters, and other females.

We must be aware that there are many circumstances over which we have no control or choice. Certainly we did not choose our race. We did not select our parents or the time we would be born. We are unable to choose what kind of disposition our children will have or how they will look. These we must accept. Acceptance is more than resignation. It is a part of our humanness to accept what we have no control over or decision in. Learning to accept others depends on how well we can accept ourselves.

As mothers we often invite heartache and frustration by being unable to accept our children for what they are; we insist that they try to be what we would like them to be. In growing to maturity we learn how to love without restrictions. We learn to love even those with whom we disagree. In the final analysis, this is the only kind of love that will bring peace to the earth.

For many years I agonized over my oldest son. His father and I had plans for him, but Bob had plans of his own. From the early age of two he had demonstrated a unique talent in music, a keenly sensitive ear, and the ability to play whatever he heard without learning the notes. As a child of three, Bob attended the University of Louisville— the youngest pupil ever accepted there. As he grew older, school began to bore him. When he was twelve, his father left a lucrative business and accepted church appointment. This resulted in an immediate transfer from our home in Kentucky to Florida. We realize now that it was a traumatic move for Bob. We were so busy with our new work that I am sure we neglected to be aware of his needs at that time.

After high school, Bob formed his own rock group. When we were transferred from the South to Ohio, Bob was unable to accept the conditions under which his father had to minister in that particular area. Although he never missed a Sunday in church up to the time he was eighteen he seldom goes now. He is a professional entertainer and an excellent musician. For years I made excuses about his way of life. Finally I grew up and learned to accept and love him as he is. It was a tremendous release for him and for me. I had always loved him as a son, but now I accept him as a human being. I go to hear him every chance I get, and I am proud that he is my son. He is a warm, lovable human being who relates well with his peers. This is not to say that I have not shared in the heartaches of a son's foolish choices, for he has made many mistakes, but I realize that everyone is entitled to make his own errors and to learn from them.

We seek to express ourselves in many ways in our home, community, at work, in the church, and with our friends. Sometimes we project an image that is totally foreign to our true natures. We act the way we think we're supposed to act rather than the way we feel. This repression is detrimental to the real identity which each of us seeks. This is not to say we aren't to discipline our lives. True discipline aids self-image. Basic to honest self-expression, however, is the understanding of self. We need to ask, What makes me feel, act, and move as I do? To what situations do I react and why? What satisfies me? What gives me a sense of well-being? What makes me happy? sad? disgruntled? Why do I flare up at some insignificant happening, but patiently endure trials and heartaches? How am I motivated? *Who am I?*

To see ourselves in the mirror of understanding will give us precise information about our aptitudes and weaknesses. It ought to help us live in accordance with our true nature—to cultivate the talents which God has given us instead of comparing ourselves with others, envying their gifts, and being thrown into despair because we feel inferior to them. We have been given special talents to be shared with the world. If we bury them or fail to develop them, we are lacking respect for God, ourselves, and mankind.

Certainly I cannot tell you how to rear your children, but I can tell you that as you seek to become human, you will find that you allow others the same privilege. We all must learn to continue together in our never ceasing search for reality in the human encounter and to express this action with each other.

Following this chapter is a series of tests which can help you determine your hostility level, your fear, guilt, hate, and inferiority feelings, *if you can be honest.* No one will see the results except you. Take a good look in this mirror and see if you can come to grips with yourself. Remember that you are not to feel blame toward anyone, including yourself. You are what you are. Accept this and go on from there. God has a purpose for your life. To live in accordance with this is normal life for you. To depart from it physically, morally, or spiritually is "wrong living" and will prevent you from celebrating your existence. You must face the conditions of your life—not as you would like them to be nor as you have been taught they should be but as they actually are. You can then set about changing them if you are dissatisfied with the self-image that you see. It is not the phony reflection in the mirror on the wall but the true image that you need to see.

Get yourself a pencil and begin writing. Then the next time you see your reflection, start smiling and enjoy the miracle of you.

You were born to become a unique, particular expression of human being. And you are the only one who can make something of your one life on earth.

—*Ross Snyder*

Tests

The following tests are taken from the book, *Prayer Can Change Your Life* by Dr. William Parker (Prentice-Hall). Used by permission of the author.

FEAR

1. When faced with a specific task, do I feel that I am too small, weak, inferior, and either not try at all or give up easily? (Fear of failure)
2. Is my reaction to normal sex relations cold, disapproving, guilty, subject to violent revulsion afterwards? (Fear of sex)
3. Do I suffer in silence while feeling that people unjustly "walk all over me"? (Fear of self-defense)
4. Am I careful never to depend on others? Do I believe that if I want something done I'd better do it myself? (Fear of trusting others)
5. Am I fearful of my own thoughts—sometimes worried by the idea that some socially unacceptable slip at the wrong time and place will ruin me? (Fear of thinking and speaking)
6. Do I constantly seek companionship, or when this is not available feel lost when some sound—radio, music, television—is not present to distract me? (Fear of being alone)

GUILT

1. Do I believe there is an "unpardonable sin," even if I cannot name it?
2. Is there a sin which I cannot personally forgive?
3. Is there anything for which I feel so deeply ashamed that I "have never mentioned it to a living soul" or never asked divine forgiveness, or having asked, kept repeating the request because I did not feel it should be granted?
4. Is there a subject which I simply refuse to discuss?
5. Do I camouflage myself when I am with people? When I am alone? Do I pretend to feel and be things which are contrary to my nature?

HATE

1. Do I want to retaliate, to "get even" with someone for a real or an imagined wrong?
2. Do I criticize? Do I build myself up by tearing others down?
3. Do I feel any satisfaction from ill news about another, even a public figure whom I do not know? (Watch this one, it's subtle.)
4. Am I overly aggressive? (Check your daily drive to the market. What kind of driver are you? Do you occupy three lanes as your right and advise everyone else how to drive? At the market do you push impatiently through and grab the

finest fruit even if it's practically from another's hand?)

5. Am I ever guilty of administering "psychological torture"? Do I enjoy it even slightly? Do I berate publicly? Humiliate? Tease? Indulge in cutting remarks?

6. Do I enjoy "taking people down a peg," putting them in their place or seeing it done to them?

INFERIORITY FEELINGS

1. Do I avoid being with others—seek to be alone rather than participate in social activities? (Seclusiveness)

2. Am I overly reserved and easily upset in the presence of others? (Self-consciousness.)

3. Am I especially sensitive to criticism or unfavorable comparison with other persons? (Sensitiveness)

4. Do I blame and criticize others, seeing in them the traits and motives I feel unworthy in myself? (Projection)

5. Do I apply to myself all unfavorable remarks and criticisms made by others? (Ideas of reference)

6. Do I try to attract attention by any method that seems likely to succeed, even if it is sometimes crude? (Attention getting)

7. Do I cover feelings of inferiority by exaggerating a desirable tendency or trait? (Compensation)

HOSTILITY TEST

How to grade this test

Score the test in the following way: look at items 5, 10, 15, 20, 25, 30. If any of these statements are marked "false," merely count them and write the number at the bottom of the test on the left-hand side. For all the other statements on the test, count those marked "true" and write this total at the bottom of the test on the right-hand side. Only two factors or traits are dealt with on this test. The two numbers at the bottom of the test represent these two factors.

The number on the left is to determine how honest you have been. If the number is 4 or above, you have not been honest with yourself. Read these items again carefully and evaluate them in the light of your past experience. Try to determine how you honestly feel, not the way you think you ought to feel. If the number is 3 or less it is safe to assume that you have answered the other statements with a fair degree of honesty. The number on the right-hand side indicates the degree of hostility (hate) you possess, whether you realize this or not. All people possess hostility. It is the degree or amount that determines the consequences. It is more detrimental if you are not aware that it is a part of you.

0-8	9-16	17-24
Not Strong	Average	Strong

Mark (T) or (F)   No. _____

1. There seems to be less love and goodwill demonstrated these days. ( )
2. Those who question the authority of the Bible are looking for an excuse to do as they please. ( )
3. Even though another person's opinion makes sense to me, I prefer to make my own decisions even though they may be wrong. ( )
4. I could name those responsible for the difficulty I have. ( )
5. I sometimes cheat at solitaire. ( )
6. Even though I like most people, there are those who do not accept me. ( )
7. It does upset me if people poke fun at me. ( )
8. Those around me seem to enjoy life more than I do. ( )
9. There have been times when all looked so bad that I had thoughts of taking my life. ( )
10. I gossip about my neighbors. ( )
11. My sexual relations have not been gratifying. ( )
12. Under certain conditions or circumstances I

feel that racial prejudice is understandable and justified. ( )

13. Many times I feel very helpless and ineffective. ( )

14. I am suspicious of people and their actions. ( )

15. When playing cards I would look at someone's hand if the opportunity presented itself. ( )

16. During the day I seem to make a great number of little mistakes. ( )

17. I am a jealous person. ( )

18. I believe that children should be spanked when they disobey. ( )

19. I often find fault with people around me. ( )

20. At times my thoughts are such that I could not tell anyone about them. ( )

21. Even my loved ones misunderstand my intentions. ( )

22. I am easily annoyed by people who do not drive properly. ( )

23. My marriage has not been as fulfilling as I would have liked. ( )

24. When people really "ask for it," I don't blame someone for giving it to them. ( )

25. I have taken things which do not belong to me. ( )

26. I am frequently annoyed by pets. ( )

27. I am sometimes sarcastic to the people around me. ( )

28. I am frequently bothered by head or stomach aches. ( )
29. Personality tests are not as valid as some believe. ( )
30. When someone has wronged me, I want to get even with them. ( )

Left Score ( )   Right Score ( )

Chapter III

CHANGE CAN BE A CHALLENGE

Probably the hardest single thing a human being has to do is learn to live successfully with change. The sameness day after day often brings a degree of false security and safety. Change, on the other hand, may breed fear and frustration. We may not agree with all that is happening in the world today, but we must be aware that we are living in a permanent state of change.

Most changes have come about during the last fifty years. All indications point to the fact that the seventies will produce even more change. A woman executive told me recently, "It seems I never actually make a change unless I am forced to do so, and then it is painful." She recognized a basic human reluctance to change and the agony involved.

The 60's have shaken us. The beautiful earth is smoke-filled and khaki-clad. Population explosion, pollution, poverty, and hunger are problems of such scope that many refuse to believe they actually exist. It is shattering for us to hear that within thirty years or less we will have no clean air to breathe anywhere on the earth unless something is done now. It is difficult to look into the face of an infant and hear the predictions of scientists that unless every family limits its offspring to two, the entire human race will be in dire trouble. It is hard for the well-clothed and well-fed (many times, overfed) to comprehend that thousands of people are starving to death daily and that two thirds of the world goes to bed hungry each night.

During the past we could perhaps wait for evolution to bring about desired change. Today we are confronted with revolution. We haven't time to wait for things to evolve . . . there must be action now! On every hand we are encompassed with those who are making their wants known by militant action, revolt, and rebellion.

The book, *Consumer of the Seventies,* contains the statement that the dimension of change in the next decade will be far greater than that experienced in any comparable period in the nation's history. Can we get ready for such changes? Can we succeed in making change a challenge?

Understanding the problems before us is relative to our own experiences. We see events and the action from where we stand. Like the six blind men who "looked" at the elephant, we see conditions from different viewpoints. If the six could have pooled their vision, they would have come up with a very different elephant—an understanding of the total rather than separated segments.

One thing is certain. We cannot stick our heads in the sand and pretend the problems will go away. Within our families, vocations, schools, churches, and communities we address change. We need to learn to live with it, profit from it, and use it productively. To do this we must view life as a mission rather than a task.

We who compose the over-thirty generation have great difficulty understanding the youth of today. Maybe we grow old rather than grow up. If we actually "grow" then we do not become old. The growth process ought to continue as long as life itself and, who knows, maybe even beyond death.

Perhaps nothing has changed as much as the part women play in society. This has come about largely since the turn of the century. Today women are also in revolt, seeking freedom to be fully human in all areas of life. A few statistics will give some idea of the changes which have already resulted.

In 1900 there were 76 million people in the United States. Today there are 200 million. In the early 1900's 30 million lived in cities with 45 million in the rural areas. Today there are 113 million in cities and only 66 million in the rural areas. In 1900 there were 56 thousand divorces while in 1960 there were 393 thousand. In the labor force in 1900 there were 5 million women. In 1960 there were 24 million. No doubt the 1970 census will tell of greater increases in all these areas.

Ninety percent of all the scientists have lived within the past sixty years. Technology is reaching a zenith. Most homes contain dozens of gadgets that bring push-button living . . . and panic probed hearts. More and more women are getting out of the house into the labor market and being criticized for it. "Woman's place is in the home" is a statement heard again and again. Why? To push buttons and turn knobs? Women need to have a choice dictated by their own desires for a life-style about working outside the home. Many do not work because they need more money but because they need opportunity for self-expression and creativity. They should be able to work without feeling guilty or odd. Many a husband still insists on being the breadwinner and head of the household. This is not reality. If a woman chooses to work outside the home, her family will not necessarily suffer. Studies indicate that married women who work because they have to upset the equilibrium of the family more than those who work because they enjoy it. Perhaps it isn't the amount of time one spends with the family but the quality of the relationship during the time spent that counts.

Today many women want to become involved in helping solve the problems of the world. Women of all ages, creeds, and color are seeking the answer to the question, "What can I do to relieve social ills?" Many do not know what to do, but the new breed of woman wants to become involved in what is going on around her. She knows that the work of today's world is beyond the back fence. She realizes that her children are not simply extensions of her own self but individuals who must be given the responsibility of choosing, and she seeks ways to assist them in making choices. Too, she is seeking a missing identity—searching for a sense of personal values interwoven with her total life. The new breed of woman thinks of her family not as an isolated unit but as a section of the world with its doors and windows open to the tensions and problems of her time. Her concern for her own children will embrace all other children.

There are three things that you, as a woman, can do to accept change as a challenge. First, take an honest look at yourself. Know who you are, where you are going, and how you are getting there. Second, abandon all limited thinking. Stop saying, "I can't" and act as if you already have. Don't look at life and ask "Why?" Say "Why not?" Don't shackle your mind with prejudiced thinking. Free your consciousness of feelings of resentment, antagonism, hate, and like emotional reactions toward others. Prepare yourself to face anything. The tempo of life today is increasing at a rapid rate. Things are unfolding almost too fast for the mind to grasp. Train yourself to be mentally alert, to keep an open mind, and to make contact with the Creator through prayer and meditation. Continue the growth process through study and involvement with all kinds of people. Cease living in the past. Make the present your concern and grow with the times. Pearl Buck has said, "The door of the house is wide open for women to walk through and into the world, but the stupendous scene beyond terrifies her." Ask yourself each morning, "What new possibility is God offering me today?"

Open the door of your house and look beyond to the world that needs your help, your response, your caring. Accept the challenge before you. Then watch yourself grow.

> *In this world a great creating and redeeming is going on. We are to participate in it. That is what life is all about.*
>
> *—Ross Snyder*

Chapter IV

WATCH THAT STRESS SYNDROME

No one can live without experiencing some degree of stress. Crossing a busy street, waiting for the light to change at an intersection, being exposed to drafts or sudden noises, vying for a bigger salary, feeling overworked, trying to stretch the food dollar, failing to bridge the communication gap, being rejected by peers, or even experiencing great joy are enough to activate the stress mechanism to some extent, depending on the situation. In fact any emotion, any activity, causes stress. But stress is not bad if the system is geared to withstand it. The same stress which makes one person sick can be an invigorating experience for another.

In his book, *Stress of Life,* Dr. Selye explains in great detail how stress affects you and how to deal with it. He says that life is largely a process of adaptation to the circumstances in which you exist. Your ability to accept or reject these circumstances could determine whether you are a healthy, happy person able to celebrate your existence or one who is constantly frustrated and ill.

49

Stress is essentially the rate of all the wear and tear caused by life. If you have ever felt that whatever you were doing, or whatever was being done to you, was strenuous and wearing, you know vaguely what is meant by stress.

The feeling of being tired, jittery, or ill is a subjective sensation of stress, and stress is not nervous tension. In fact, stress reactions can occur in the lower animals which do not even have nervous systems. Stress is a state manifested by a syndrome. It is not stress that causes an alarm reaction; it is the stressor (the event, the pressure) that does. The state of stress in a person can be appraised by the changes it produces. When a rubber band is stretched taunt, it is in a state of tension, but this is recognizable only by physical changes in the rubber.

Dr. Selye's postulation that all disease comes as a result of chemical imbalance within the system caused by stress may indeed have merit. He states that in all his practice he has yet to see a person die of old age. Death resulting from old age would mean that all parts of the body have worn out at one time, and this is not the case. People die because one part fails to function, or is stressed to the exhaustion point.

There are three components of stress: (1) the alarm reaction caused by the stressor, (2) a stage of resistance when the body or mind puts up a struggle against the stress, and (3) the stage of exhaustion, which is fatigue resulting in rest, or in some cases, death.

Stress is usually the outcome of a struggle for self-preservation of parts within the whole. This is true of individual cells within man, of man within society, and of individual species within the whole animate world. Everybody tries to project a good image, to be accepted by others, to achieve success and attain fame and fortune. One of the doctor's favorite quotes is:

> Fight always for the highest attainable aim,
> But never put up resistance in vain.

Have you ever tried hard to change a situation, knowing all the time that your efforts were futile? No doubt this resulted in great stress to your entire body and mind.

Stress is a three-pronged instrument: (1) the stressor, that external agent which starts the trouble by acting directly on a part of the body or mind; (2) the defensive measure, such as the hormones and nervous stimuli which encourage the body to defend itself against the stressor as well as it can (mental stressors—i.e. orders, challenges, offenses are met with corresponding complex emotional defensive responses); and (3) the mechanisms for surrender such as hormonal and nervous stimuli which encourage the body *not* to defend itself. For example, in order not to put up defense, but to ignore emotional stressors, one needs deviation. Something must be put in its place. All work and no play is not good, but what is work for one is play for another. It is sufficient to change one's daily schedule in some way which will relieve the stress for a time. Delays are costly.

The person who is refused the right of self-expression—of doing his own thing, as it were—will ultimately find himself a product of the third phase of stress. For a time his body will fight back (stage No. 2), but unless his stress quotient is very high and he can hold out indefinitely or give in to the third stage (rest), he will fall prey to disease and mental illnesses.

We all have varying degrees of love and hate. Actually we can treat our enemies one of two ways. We can love them, or we can hate them. If we choose the latter, we open up a can of woes for ourselves that will bring more grief than we can handle. Dr. Selye thinks gratitude and revenge are key words relative to stress and our lives. Hate breeds revenge, and revenge spawns stress that no one can sustain without serious ill effects to both body and mind. The Great Teacher knew exactly what he was talking about when he said we should love our enemies and do good for evil. There is tremendous power in being able to sincerely effect these feelings for people who misuse us; it brings the other side of the coin into play—the healing qualities of gratitude.

Gratitude is the awakening in another the wish that I should prosper because of what I have done for him. In short, by inspiring the feeling of gratitude, I induce another person to share with me my natural wish for my own well-being. Upon this principle rests peace of mind, feelings of security or insecurity, fulfillment or frustration.

Revenge is the awakening in another the wish that I should *not* prosper because of what I have done to him. It is the most important threat to security. It also has its roots in a natural defense reaction. When we punish a child for doing something bad, our action comes very close to revenge. Punishment is an object lesson which teaches proper future conduct by retaliation. We must be very careful to use it properly. Perhaps this is why so many modern educators are against the idea of punishment.

Both gratitude and revenge are rewards. When we are bad we are punished, and when we are good we receive reward. But revenge hurts both the giver and receiver. It generates more revenge, while gratitude tends to incite more gratitude. Think for a moment how you feel when you have done something for someone you like, and you are thanked and appreciated. Now do the same thing for your enemy or one whom you dislike and with whom you disagree. Doesn't it bring the same feelings of appreciation?

Gratitude is a guide to conduct which avoids stress in interpersonal relations and gives us more freedom to enjoy life's wonders. We all need the satisfaction which comes from contemplating the wonders of creation. We want and need the joy and pleasures our senses can bring. In our effort to secure them, we will use one of the two described methods—gratitude or revenge. Gratitude, whether received or given, is in itself a very enjoyable feeling.

I have seen a group of young people who had been rejected by a certain congregation literally love those who rejected them into acceptance. If this is successful on a small scale, couldn't it be used to bring peace and love to the entire world?

When we experience a period of stress, alarm signals are sent out by stressed tissues including the mind. The pituitary and adrenals produce adaptive hormones which combat wear and tear in both. When we go past our stress quotient, delaying the final stage of fatigue or rest, breakdown occurs. Each person needs to find his optimum stress level and then use the adaptation energy at a rate and in a direction adjusted to the structure of the mind and body. Adaptation energy seems to be something of which everybody has a certain amount at birth.

As women we have yet to learn how to cope with today's stresses. To a great extent our survival depends on it. A person who is ill mentally, physically, or emotionally sees life through grey-colored glasses and will never be able to celebrate existence. We were created to see the beauty of all things, including our own lives.

I suggest that you read Dr. Selye's book for a greater understanding of this problem. I have given only a brief glimpse but enough—I hope—to cause you to want to know more.

> *Now here [said the Red Queen] it takes all the running you can do to keep in the same place. If you want to get somewhere else, you must run at least twice as fast as that!—Lewis Carroll*

Chapter V

ARE YOU A COPOUT?

Have you ever felt like screaming, "Stop the world. I want to get off"? I have. I think there are times in every life when it becomes too much and we want to cop out. These are temporary situations and serve as a safety valve for our tensions and frustrations. This chapter deals with another kind of copout which I believe is what happens when we refuse to live up to our potential as human beings.

Despite the hippies and yippies and other segments of society that have been accused of turning off, history may record that in the last half of the twentieth century, women were actually the biggest copouts of the age.

Comprising 52 percent of the total U. S. population and controlling 75 percent of the wealth of the nation, women—many of them at least—have relegated themselves to keeping house, fulfilling their duties and desires in the bedroom, and producing an overpopulated earth. Please don't misunderstand. I'm all for a woman being a wife and mother. I insist, however, that she owes far more responsibility to living than what those few years grant her.

A good deal is said about women's rights today. (I like the term "responsibilities" better.) None of us want our sons killed and maimed in war . . . but are we willing to pay the price for peace? It's difficult to find clean air, yet how many of us are engaged in seeking ways to end the pollution of the environment? We're sick of the sex image projected on tube and screen—or are we? We insist we'd like to shut Madison Avenue up, but we continue responding to its gimmicks, buying its products, and making ourselves sick because we're not like the models in the ads. We know we must have better schools, but how many of us are willing to qualify and run for school board positions? We are constantly shouting about youth and the drug abuses, but a look in our medicine cabinets reveals that we ourselves are addicted. We take pep pills to give us energy, tranquilizers to keep our nerves steady, and sleeping pills for a restful night.

We complain that we're tired of being stuck with certain jobs in the labor market, but how many of us have the fortitude to break the male-oriented society by qualifying for roles as judges, physicians, lawyers, politicians, scientists? We're really uptight about our problems with our siblings, but how many of us are willing to go through the agony of opening our minds and really listening to what they are telling us?

The woman copout wraps up her whole life in her children and domesticity. She has a hard time adjusting to the constant change going on around her and an even harder time letting the siblings go from the nest. She messes up her own future, dominates her spouse, and alienates her progeny. She has never seen herself as a personality, an individual in her own right, so she has trouble recognizing young people as individuals instead of carbon copies. She is the feminine mystique, all right, but the greatest mystery remains unsolved because she refuses to come down from her ivory tower and become aware of the potential within her.

There is a dismal future for those who turn off or tune out today. To become aware of the life around one is to expose oneself to all the hurts and heartaches of society. But to pretend they do not exist or that they'll simply go away if ignored is to refuse one's birthright as a human being.

Several years ago I watched a woman grieve over the death of her fifteen-year-old daughter. The girl was a beautiful promise of an outstanding life, and it was a senseless death. The woman had other children, but losing this one child was a bitter blow. For several years she hardly knew what to do with herself. Finally in desperation she forced herself to an understanding of life. Today she is a counselor for juvenile girls who are on probation from the courts. She confessed to me, "It wasn't easy, and at times I nearly quit. There were long training sessions, and I felt so inadequate, but I kept on." This has made a big difference in her life. She has grown emotionally and continues to grow as she suffers with these girls who have lost their way. She is thrilled when she can help them readjust to society. Although the hurts of such burdens are constantly with her, she is growing to a new and wonderful maturity because of it. She is a human being helping herself and others.

How many women take other people's unwanted children into their homes and hearts while they are awaiting adoption? Not nearly enough, the agencies tell us. These children, many of them infants, need love and care. This is a marvelous outreach for any woman whose children are grown but who retains the need of maternal fulfillment.

Angie Brooks, Liberian president of the United Nations General Assembly, has educated and cared for 47 children, 19 of whom are still under her care at this time. What a tremendous contribution she has made in this field alone.

Many a woman actually believes that the male is superior to her. If he is top on the totem pole, he is also responsible for the mess the world is in. This attitude relieves women of the burden.

We spend years playing with the babies and the house. But babies grow up and become adults and we can't play with them any longer. The house becomes our cage, and we are afraid to break out. When we reach fifty, we wake up and wonder where the magic went. We have allowed our minds to become stale and our intellect to atrophy from lack of use. We may even find ourselves living with strangers who look at us across the breakfast table without really knowing who or what they see.

When a couple who have been married thirty or forty years break up, we shake our heads and ask why. What happens between two people who have shared bed and board for so many years? Could it possibly be that one or the other or maybe both have grown old mentally as well as physically and cease to be aware of life?

What's the answer? I'm not about to give you a formula for what you can do to fulfill yourself as a whole human being equipped to function all of life and not just part of it. But if you don't want to be labeled a copout you'll discover the answer (everyone's different). I don't know what the future holds for you, but I do know this: only those who have found the ability to serve will be happy.

Women have a role to play which outdistances the role of wife and mother. These are very important, but until a woman becomes aware of her own potential as a human being, she isn't even an adequate wife or mother. Children are given for mothers to love, provide for, assist in growing to maturity, and cut loose. They must be allowed the freedom to become.

Statistics point out that you'll outlive your husband. Medical science is providing the opportunity for a long life, with good health, for you. What do you intend to do with the last half of your life? Look about you. There's a world out there. One thing it doesn't need is another copout. It is filled with exciting, creative ways to enrich all of life. Accept your responsibility as a woman with courage, faith, and the willingness to fulfill the tremendous potential that is yours. Go on, take the step. And keep on keeping on:

> *We are alive only in the moment of some*
> *fresh birthing of ourselves. We are alive*
> *in some growing edge of our lives.*
> —Ross Snyder

Chapter VI

THE OPEN CIRCLE

We live in an impersonal world, yet it is made up of persons. Actually we live in two worlds—one of things and one of persons. The trouble is we use people and love things instead of the other way around. We may see life as nothing but things. Mechanisms, art, philosophy, and religion can also become things, collections of concepts, definitions. On the other hand, we can open ourselves to a world of persons. The person refuses to be confined within concepts and definitions. It is not a thing to be encompassed but a point of attraction, an attitude which demands from us a corresponding attitude, which moves us to action and commits us. The world of things does not commit us; it is neutral. It is the person that has meaning, a birth and an end. To many, people have become pawns on the chessboard, cogs, learning machines to be manipulated. One of the worst sins of modern life is the sin of manipulating people. We need to open our eyes to the world of persons. As we do this, animals, plants, and even inanimate things take on the quality of persons. We need to be more interested in people as persons than in their ideas, their party labels, the color of their skin, or the way they say their prayers. This means a complete thought revolution for changing the climate of our lives.

People are lonely and frustrated because they are separated from God and from each other. It is a loneliness not of space but of spirit. The problem is not separation of distance but of souls, a polarization of spirits. We are divided from each other by the separateness of our psychic organism, by what has influenced us in tradition, history, and environment. We are also divided within ourselves.

Human personality is at once the best known and least understood of all forms of existence. Each woman knows herself best from inside information of her own experience and what it means for her to live through it. She can feel her own shadings of mood from moment to moment. Yet there are shadowy unknowns in the unconscious depths of her nature that impel or restrain her in a baffling interplay of conflicting tendencies. Thus, each woman becomes a problem to herself. She may start to act, then hesitate and come to a standstill while she ponders the situation. Especially when she has been hurt by another person or institution, it is extremely easy for her to erect a barrier to withstand further hurts and very difficult to allow herself once more to become open and vulnerable. Through centuries, walls have been erected between people, races, and nations. It is no small matter to tear these down, but down they must come as the circle opens to the whole world of persons.

The rising tide of mental breakdowns and the mounting suicide rates indicate that thousands of lonely souls are finding life too unbearable, too frustrating, too full of hurts. Yet we were created to live in harmony with the universe. Reconciliation, which is the harmony of all things, is desperately needed if we are to survive. Love, then, is required to untangle human relations. But what is love? And how do we love? Where can we find the ability to be compassionate with those who connect daily with us within the family unit, the neighborhood, the church, in civic affairs, in the world of business? People are so very different. Communication is so extremely difficult. It is so easy to withdraw into our small circle because it is safe and secure. Yet the human race must find a way to be yoked together in the involvement of life if it is to survive. We must love or perish!

What does your circle encompass? What kind of involvement do you have in the lives of others? It takes skill to become involved with other people's problems and not get personally confused. How many black people do you know well enough to disagree with? What about Mexican-Americans, Indians, and other ethnic groups? These people have so much to offer from their culture that you will miss one of life's great opportunities if you do not seek them out and make friends of them. I do not mean merely sitting next to them in the church or on a bus. I'm talking about living in the same neighborhoods, going to the same schools, belonging to the same clubs, working side by side.

Have you ever watched small children play? They have no prejudices except as they are taught them by adults. I recall an occasion when my five-year-old granddaughter was visiting us from Florida. One evening while she was there a young black couple with their five children visited us. Robin and the other children went off to play immediately. No introductions were necessary. Her father told me later that she had never before had an opportunity to play with black children. Though Robin lives many miles from us, whenever we see these children they ask first, "How's Robin?"

The open circle is a people-to-people relationship regardless of race, creed, or social standing. It is mutual concern born out of the knowledge that God is no respecter of persons and has indeed "made of one blood all nations." How very tragic to see people claiming a God who selects one kind of people from within his universe to be the recipient of his favor while condemning unborn generations with a curse. How God must weep to see his creation so lacking in understanding and knowledge of him. The so-called Christian has done much damage by condoning segregation and allowing himself to be caught up in the white supremacy power structure.

Let me tell you about Katie. She came from Uganda to the United States for a three-month tour. When we first met, we immediately sensed a mutual bond of friendship even though our worlds were quite different. During her visit here, Katie became ill and had to be hospitalized. Many people were kind to her. A simple get-well card which carried a verse by St. Francis of Assisi found within her heart a unique meaning. It was her favorite verse—and mine. We became good friends, interested in each other's family, country, opinion, and beliefs. When Katie returned to Uganda, we continued our friendship through correspondence. Though it is doubtful that we shall ever meet again, I consider getting to know her one of the beautiful experiences of my life. She, along with other black people whom I have met in my work, have enabled me to understand and respect the black community and to appreciate its contribution to the world. It is part of my open circle.

Are you aware that the rich also constitute a minority group? One of my best friends is rich. She is a very real person both to the poor and the middle-class. I don't feel ill at ease in her presence, nor do I envy her because she has wealth. She is a very generous person. Yet there are those who are jealous of this woman, who feel that her wealth sets her apart. Because of their attitude they deny themselves the friendship of a warm human being.

Open your circle to include people of all races and creeds. You will find a whole new adventure awaiting you as you learn from them and share the same sorrows, laugh over the same mistakes, have the same dreams and hopes. Create within yourself the ability really to listen to others and you'll discover, though you may never agree with them, that you understand them and are drawn to them. I remember hearing a black militant on television. I decided that I would listen with my whole heart to what he was saying. As he poured out his soul about the plight of his people I found myself feeling with him, and the beginning of understanding started to dawn. Not that I agreed with his methods, but I did understand his motives and I found myself rethinking the whole problem of the black people.

Remember the story about walking in another's

shoes? It may be the only way to bring reconciliation to the human race.

One other thing . . . widen your circle to include people of all ages. The youth of today are so alive. Their vitality can add a dimension to your life that you'll find nowhere else. You can relate to them if you display a sincere concern and love for them and their problems. They will respond with affection and make you feel years younger. As you grow older, your friends will die and you'll need new friends to replace them. You either make new friends and widen the circle or close it up completely and withdraw from society.

Integration of the whole human race must come if there is ever to be peace. It begins with you and me and each person whose life touches ours. There's an entire company of persons out there whose lives never touch anyone or anything except misery and loneliness. They need you! Broaden your circle, and keep it open. You'll discover it pays big dividends.

> *Caring is your energies mobilized, interfused with deep feeling, engaged with the world—and it makes a difference to you how it comes out.—Ross Snyder*

Chapter VII

STOP! LOOK! LISTEN!

Life goes by so fast. Stop a moment and take a look at it. You've probably heard this before, but have you really been aware of what it means?

We take so little time to get to know each other, much less ourselves. To be aware of life and all that it encompasses is perhaps the chief virtue lacking in our society today. We look but do not see. We hear but do not listen. And our own distorted lives reflect this vital need. We are so busy going nowhere that when we arrive we are bewildered and miss completely the joy of achieving our somewhat nebulous destination.

What do you believe in? Yourself? Your country? Your education? The structure of this society? God? Then what do you disbelieve in? Yourself? Your country? Your neighbor? Your God? Everyone believes or disbelieves in certain values, people, things. Some never bother to discover what they believe. Many only doubt.

The scriptural admonition to "be still and know" has never been more relevant than in our present world. Do you ever talk to God? You may call it prayer. I call it dialogue because I feel it is a two-way conversation. Are you honest in your dialogue with him? We can fool others, and even ourselves a good deal of the time, but we can never fool the Creator because he made us, and knows us better than we know ourselves. He listens when we speak. We need to tune our hearts to listen to his reply.

Many persons are never still long enough to make contact with God until some earth-shaking catastrophe forces them to their knees. Then they cry "Why?"

There is at work in our world a force which can produce a calm, undaunted spirit in the midst of turmoil and unrest. This is the energy of prayer. In order to be able to pray effectively we need periods of meditation and contemplation each day. The perfunctory good-night prayer is not sufficient for the hectic lives most of us lead. Continued long enough it will only lead to doubt and misgivings. Praying only when we are in trouble or pain makes God a mere errand boy who sits around waiting for us to stumble and fall before need for him arises. This is not God's nature or function. The story is told of an ocean liner sinking. As the huge vessel was going under people began frantically falling on their knees praying for help. One man stood quietly at the rail, looking out over the water. Some rushed up to him and said, "Aren't you going to join us in prayer?" "No," he quietly replied, "I have spent my life praying, and I am ready for this moment." Disciplined prayer which acknowledges a two-way communication between the Creator and us, with our becoming subservient to him, will enable us to endure anything life has to offer and remain victorious. This is an art which must be learned. It takes a lifetime of practice, devotion, and discipline.

Augustine said that man is restless until he rests in God. He also said that every Christian should be an alleluia from head to foot. In other words, we should celebrate our existence and shout praises about it. The spirit of prayer and meditation leads us to dream and plan and strive. In prayer and contemplation we see quite simple things in our lives which our intelligence has failed to perceive. We also are inspired to act, for life is made up of an alternation between meditation and action. Action prepared in meditation is quite different in quality from the hectic, breathless activity which characterizes our age, filling it with noise, agitation, and frenzy and which is one of the chief causes of the increased incidence of nervous disorders.

We urgently need spiritual transformation, but a spiritual revolution of our lives will not come unless we stop in our tracks and honestly examine the hectic course of our thoughts and activities. Spiritual renewal comes only by meeting God face-to-face. In spite of our good intentions, in spite of our knowledge, in spite of our advanced technology, there are difficulties in our lives that cannot be overcome by effort of the will, problems that cannot be solved by exercise of reason, faults that time cannot erase. We all need a place and a time to be alone with God, alone to face ourselves as we are, as we have been, and as we wish to be.

If we can become aware of who we are in this process of contemplation we shall also become aware of others. We'll learn to understand them as we learn to understand ourselves, and we'll be concerned. We'll discover that we need each other. Truly, "No man is an island, no man stands alone." The human race is bound together by ties deeper than family or nationality. We can gain insight into deleterious actions, including our own, and seek ways to avoid erecting such barriers. The energy and creative wonder of the universe is blended in each of us; we are all a part of a magnificent Whole.

When we sense the sweep of God's love for us and indeed for all mankind a light is cast on our own condition, revealing us to ourselves as no amount of introspection can do. Pascal calls this a chamber of loving scrutiny, able to bring self-realization which can banish trouble from our lives. If we can stay in this chamber long enough, aware of our shortcomings, we can receive the revelation of what must be put right and the strength to put it right.

Because of the accelerated pace at which we live today, it is essential that we find time for meditation. If we neglect this, we are failing to take advantage of one of life's greatest releases. We should set apart a time and a place each day where we can be alone in quietness. We are constantly bombarded with noise. Scientists now tell us that the noise pollution is second only to the air pollution and that the toll is just as deadly. When we walk down a busy street or stand in a crowded store we get the feeling that everyone is uptight. Tense reverberations are everywhere. People want peace of mind, but not the ivory-tower escapism which leads to excesses. The kind of peace we need comes only one way. We must learn the art of unwinding daily through contact with the Source of all life.

Some women seem to be busy all the time, rushing from one activity to another with apparent ease. Often this is their flight into activity to avoid confrontation with themselves, their lives, and their purpose in being. The person who is busy with important tasks will realize the need to "be still and know."

Private and corporate worship helps prevent

serious hang-ups, but worship must be meaningful and relevant to the present. If we believe in God, we will want to meditate daily on his goodness to us and enlist his aid in making those decisions which face us at every turn. Many youth who experiment with drugs do so because they are seeking a meaningful experience with someone or something outside themselves. Many are finding they can realize the fulfillment of this search in God and Christ.

Nature abhors a vacuum. Unless we place within our mind—both the one-tenth that we use and the nine-tenths subconscious—those positive, revitalizing thoughts, the little negative, poisonous seeds will take root and grow.

Can you set apart fifteen minutes or a half-hour a day to be alone? Perhaps a poem, a favorite scripture or reading, a beautiful painting, or your special record may assist you to get started. True contemplation, of course, is best done in silence. Once you've established such a pattern you'll find your life taking on a new dimension, and not only will you be able to celebrate your existence but you'll discover that all people will have a special meaning to you.

> *If contemplation, which introduces us to the very heart of creation, does not inflame us with such love that it gives us,*

together with deep joy, the understanding of the infinite misery of the world, it is a vain kind of contemplation. The sign of true contemplation is charity (love). By your capacity for forgiveness shall I recognize your God, and also by your opening your arms to all creation.—Marius Grout

Chapter VIII

RISK THE IMPOSSIBLE

We live in a day when the status quo is not acceptable or adequate for the future of man. There must come innovation, change, risk. Innovation is more than a new method—it's a wholly new view of the universe. It encompasses a fresh look at man's role in the scheme of things. Risk is more than simply taking a chance—it is standing on the periphery. Order is created by taking risks and by assuming the responsibility for those risks.

We are still saying to our youth, "Listen, and take our advice." We need to be saying to them, "Strive with us so that together we can create a new world." We must listen to them, for they are trying desperately to tell us about their hopes and dreams and ideals.

In the past people could shrug their shoulders in the face of most of the evils of life because they were powerless to prevent them. Today we have only ourselves to blame. Anything is possible; everything can be accomplished. The decision is up to us and must be deliberately made. The fate of mankind depends on what we choose to do.

To live in fear of moving to bring a new order is

to choose suicide for the race. There is more knowledge and information available today than ever before, but this knowledge can become a prison rather than liberation. Knowledge must be conquered much as the wilderness of pioneer days.

Someone has said that the new frontier is the mind itself. If we will open our eyes to the world around us, we shall see that risk is what it's all about.

One of my favorite Bible stories is the account of Joshua and Caleb and their impossible dream. Moses had led the children of Israel to the edge of Canaan, their promised land. There they rested while twelve men were sent to reconnoiter the land. Ten of these men came back filled with fear and said to the people, "We can't take this land . . . it's full of giants." But Joshua and Caleb—two young men full of vigor, youth, and faith—brought back a different picture. Carrying a huge cluster of grapes on their shoulders, they told the people, "Here is a land flowing with milk and honey. Let us go forward as the Lord has commanded." But the people listened to the ten cowards. They were afraid to risk the unknown even with their dream just before them. For forty years they wandered in the wilderness, and only those who were under twenty-one at the time were allowed to enter Canaan when Joshua led them to victory. The history of the entire Jewish race might have been different had these people been willing to risk the impossible. They were standing on the edge of their tomorrow, but they turned their backs on it for the wandering of the present. How long have we been wandering in the wilderness of hate, greed, and fear?

Faith is not the absence of fear but the mastery of it—the ability to take a stand, to dare the impossible, to go out on a limb even though the limb may be severed. It's the business of the true Christian to be risky. Risk is not taking a chance or gambling. Risk is caring deeply about something and being willing to work for it even when the outcome isn't sure. Mr. Snyder believes risk is diving into life twenty fathoms deep.

Today all humanity hangs in the balance. The many problems confronting us grow more momentous day by day. Dissent has always been part of human nature, yet when dissent turns to violence and in turn breeds violence whereby innocent people are killed, one must ask, "Why?" and shout, "Enough!"

Today the cry is for peace. Young people are filled with despair at the thought of their future in a world where war exists. They feel a hopelessness that we adults cannot fathom. Are we willing to risk everything for peace, or is peace too much a part of that impossible dream and therefore unattainable?

A sociology professor at a west Michigan university confessed that he foresaw man returning to a savage state if the present trend continues. Unless he is willing to seek direction from a Higher Power and follow wherever it leads it may well be that the man of tomorrow will be that savage.

How willing are we to lay aside our hostilities and resentments, our hang-ups about conformity and tradition to ensure a society where everyone is counted for himself? War, poverty, loss of dignity and freedom must cease if man is to see his dream fulfilled. Love is the only antidote. It begins in the life of each individual as he relates to another human being. It begins in the family unit as each recognizes the intrinsic worth of the other as a person of value. It starts when we desire the same fulfillment of basic needs for all people, not just part of society, and are willing to risk all to accomplish this.

We cry for garments of love to be woven for us in our everyday lives. We long to love and be loved. Yet even loving involves risk. We expose ourselves to pain and vulnerability.

If Christianity has failed, it isn't because of its Founder. It is because those who profess to follow him are unable to love as he commanded and demonstrated in his unique living and dying. The life of this Man from Nazareth proves beyond a shadow of a doubt that other men can love, can risk, and can be alive. They can forgive their enemies and do good for evil. It is possible for them to love without restrictions.

Risk begins with small things. It is the willingness to allow courage to overcome fear. I recall one occasion when my youngest son was home on leave from the Air Force. He had a small sports car and wanted me to ride home with him one evening. Previously I had been unable to muster up enough courage to get in it and roar off down the highway. This time I said to myself, "Why not? All that can possibly happen is an accident. I could die. But," I reasoned, "it will do a great deal for John. He will know I trust him." So I rode with him . . . and discovered that I wasn't even afraid. In fact, I rather enjoyed it. Result: the demise of one hang-up.

Faith is not the absence of fear but the mastery of it. If the goal ahead is peace on earth, then as women we must risk our total lives in pursuit of it. This means involvement and commitment. It also means consistency with what we preach. Sometimes it might mean loneliness. Shaping our environment to allow for peace requires right relations with each other and with God. Peace will come when enough people care and are consistent with the principles of peace in the living of their daily lives. Peace cannot come by force any more than love can. Peace and love are woven of the same cloth, and reconciliation is the tender thread which binds them together. Right now peace seems an impossible dream. We must be willing to risk whatever is necessary to bring this dream to pass.

> *Risk is taking on a real battle, a real engagement. It is exposing one's self to possible hurt "for the sake of." Moments of risk are times of aliveness. The world could stand more of this from us.—Ross Snyder*

Chapter IX

ON THE EDGE OF TOMORROW

Down through the centuries of time men have sought to live in community, for they were created to be a part of their environment and of each other. No human being has ever lived who hasn't longed for a world of peace and plenty—a utopia of some sort. Many have tried strange combinations hoping to reach their impossible dream, but it has remained just that—impossible. Abraham left his home and friends to seek a city whose builder and maker was God. Jesus looked over Jerusalem and wept because the people were not ready to gather in community as he longed for them to do.

Man has never been willing to follow the pattern with enough fidelity to assure the building of such a society. Yet the pattern has been before him a long time. Jesus was the kingdom in an individual mold. He said to his followers, "The kingdom of heaven is within you." If we study his life we'll discover how to build a kingdom of peace within ourselves which will result in the impossible dream becoming reality. The scriptures speak of a time "when every man shall sit under his own fig tree, and none shall make him afraid." I believe that time is almost here. We are standing on the edge of tomorrow.

It is true that the world is filled with unrest. Problems and tensions seem insurmountable, and technological advances merely add to the burden of man's loneliness. What many dreamers and planners of utopias have failed to understand is that one cannot legislate the hearts of men to love their fellows. No courts can force another to love, for love is of the heart. There is arising today out of the turmoil and turbulence abroad in the world a movement toward community for all men. Marshall McLuhan has convinced us that we live in a global village. Electricity has brought the entire world into our living room. What happens to people in India, China, and Russia now becomes meaningful to me, and in the process of becoming human and learning to celebrate my existence, I find my concern for others paramount to my own well-being and happiness.

The groaning and pain we hear is the earth struggling to be reborn, possible only as man himself finds rebirth. If we stretch hard, standing on tiptoe, we'll be able to see the beginning.

History records a people who had perfect right relationships with God and with each other. They were called Zion. They were of one heart and one mind, and there were no poor among them. Being of one heart and mind does not mean there was no diversity, but there was unity in diversity. The purpose was all for one—that of loving God, their neighbor, and themselves—people living in community for each other.

It is difficult to conceive of a world where there is no poverty. Thousands die daily from neglect and malnutrition. This suggests a tremendous barrier between the haves and the have-nots. But the gap is narrowing. We are becoming aware that poverty must be eliminated, that we cannot be human and live in plenty while our brother lives in want. The barrier is coming down as the love of God evidenced by man to man strips away the veneer and pretense and we become acutely aware of all human potential. This is not to suggest that all people will have the same amount of goods or resources. It does mean that all will have their needs, just wants, and the opportunity to fulfill their potential and purpose in existence with dignity and freedom.

Today we have walked on the moon. Tomorrow we shall walk in splendor on the earth, for the earth is man's habitation. While we have defiled it, polluted it, and misused it, we have finally been awakened to the need for displaying stewardship for all life, including the earth.

Whether or not we choose to recognize it, we are

stewards over all life. Mission is why we are here. Understood, this can ensure an atmosphere for our becoming human and aware of our heritage. We will then be able to bring about the kingdom of peace and plenty for all. Our society has been so hung-up on politics, procedures, regulations, and rules that we have ceased to be human beings concerned about one another. Computers did not dehumanize man—they merely pointed up the inhumanity which already existed. Force can never change our hearts, but we do have at our fingertips the resources and ability to achieve this love we so desperately desire.

Once we understand ourselves we can move to understand and identify with others. When we encompass the celestial law, which is the law of love, the kingdom of God will come on the earth, even as it is in heaven.

A young man at Yale University said recently that the new world was going to be built not by tearing down the old but by building above it. Then, he felt, people would see the new order and respond to it. There are thousands of young men and women of vision and vitality who are standing on the edge of tomorrow ready to take the leap to fulfillment of their dreams.

Certainly youth is in rebellion. The whole world is in the throes of revolution. New values and priorities must be set because man has failed to find his true purpose with the old values. This big, beautiful earth created for his inheritance must be given the opportunity to claim fulfillment, and man himself must discover his purpose in being. Centuries of veneer must be stripped away so that he can see his humanness, a part of which is divine, and seeing respond to the life-style of the kingdom.

We can hasten this day by realizing who we are and our reason for being. We can come to grips with the fact that the world is changing, and we can help direct these changes by accepting responsibility for existing as human beings—and more importantly, being women with tremendous potential and power.

Dignity and freedom have to be restored to all men who now walk in disparity and chains, for freedom is inherent in the human soul—freedom to become, to choose, to love and to be loved. This is the quest, the secret longing, of everyone, for it brings the freedom to be. Although it may be difficult for us to see the millennium ahead because of the Armageddon through which we are now passing, we may be assured that it shall come. Robert Kennedy said, "The future does not belong to those who are content with today; rather it will belong to those who can blend vision, reason, and courage in a personal commitment." The peace of the world is cast in the frontiers of our hearts from where it must spread to the limits of the universe.

We are standing on the edge of that tomorrow, and we must build, build, build!

> *The universe in which we are placed has been in travail toward the emergence of a world network of thinking men, deeply caring about each other, in honest communication with each other, each open to the lure of God to become more than he now is.* — *Ross Snyder*

Chapter X

REJOICE, YOU'RE ALIVE!

An eight-year-old boy attended the funeral of a good friend. He felt a lack of concern among those present. He later remarked to his mother, "Some people live; others just pump blood." Joe Braun voiced a great truth.

What is living? Can you feel your heart beating? If so, you're alive, but are you really living? Living means embracing all of life, meeting it head on, being vital and aware. Apathy has no meaning for one who is alive. Each day becomes a challenge, another mountain to climb. The heart is a magnificent machine. If it breaks down, attempts to use a substitute over any extended period of time cause complications and often death.

Do you believe in miracles? They happen all the time. Today, try looking for a miracle. Regardless of what else may be wrong, or the problems you have to solve, just for now be happy because you are alive and breathing. Celebrate your existence!

A good friend of mine in her early sixties always replies with great vigor to the perfunctory, "How are you today?" "I'm just fine," she replies. Everyone believes her, and few are aware of the times she is in pain or has burdens. She is a vibrant human being. When greeted by "Have a good day," one young man I know always remarks, "All my days are good!" And he means it.

Actually these are affirmative mind teasers which have a therapeutic effect on both the speaker and the listener. You are what you think. The positive approach to life guarantees that a person can stay alive all of his life.

"Rejoice, you're alive," means, "This is the day the Lord has made. We will rejoice and be glad in it." *This is the day!* What other commodity in your life is worth as much as your time? It is your most valuable stewardship. Don't be careless with it. Everyone has the same number of hours in each day. This is perhaps the only real equality people have.

So you've discovered life isn't a bowl of cherries? Cherries have pits, you know. Burdens and problems are the cisterns of growth for humanity. The ability to transcend trials distinguishes the successful people from the dropouts. Failure won't hurt you if you use it as a stepping-stone. Regardless of your inability to reach a goal, if you try, the venture is successful.

Doctors say that 75 percent of all patients who frequent their offices are suffering from psychosomatic illnesses. This does not mean they are not ill or in pain. It does mean that the mind and emotions are responsible for the affliction, and some psychic problem is the chief culprit. Migraines, ulcers, functional heart trouble, backaches, asthma, arthritis, and many other diseases can be traced to hostility and resentment. The patient who frees himself of these demons can become a beautiful, happy, turned-on person.

Are you interested in new things? Life is a process of becoming. To continue growing and becoming, you must keep mentally and emotionally pliable by getting excited about new things, new activities, new friends, new ideas. If you are doing the same things year after year, reading the same books, seeing the same people, thinking the same thoughts, you can be sure that rigor mortis has already set in. Venture out in your life and seek new forms of self-expression. Try to develop your mind. The glory of God is intelligence or light and truth. Discover the miracle of living.

For too long Christianity has been placed on a shelf between bookends of long-faced do's and don't's. The Christian must break from this cocoon like the butterfly and discover the real Christianity. Religion is a dimension of life if it is experienced in a meaningful way. It is the only dimension which can bring hope out of utter hopelessness. It cannot be divided into the sacred and the secular. It is a way of life. It is all of life. Discover what religion can do and the freedom it can bring.

Celebrating life requires a special way of seeing, of discovering. If you desire more cleaning power out of your dishwasher, put more cleaning power in it. Realize that there's a world out there, a real "make it work" world. Each day you experience all the little ordinary joys if you are aware and respond to life. Look at the beauty of a sunset, the texture of bread, the smoothness of glass, the pattern of moonlight on the water, birds in flight, a waterfall, the eyes of a child. Life goes by so fast. Stop for a moment and look at it. Take time to express your concern about others as you relate to them and identify with them.

Jesus said, "I have come that you might have life and have it more abundantly." But people are afraid to accept his gift and respond to his way. You are alive as you respond to life. Thousands of people just exist . . . just "pump blood." Comparatively few have found the secret of abundant living. Fear and foibles restrict. Today's woman must adapt to the change around her, or she will break under the strain. As a woman living in today's world you are one of three and one-half billion human beings. As an American you live in a nation with one hundred and four million other women. During your life you play many roles, but each one can bring wisdom and grace if you so will. And you can live all of your life in joy.

Childhood can be a beautiful time. A child holds no grudges, harbors no hate. But when we become adults, we proudly put away childish things. We put away our childish faith, our wonder, and our love. We clothe ourselves with adult hostilities and fears. We create monsters in our mirrors. Jesus once said we must become as little children in order to enter his kingdom. A child is filled with awe as he sees even the simple things in life. He is eager to learn. He is alive. Could this be what the Master meant? Children cry when they hurt. We're ashamed to weep. They respond to love and affection. We hide our emotions and are self-conscious about our feelings. Children are honest. Our lives are covered with veneer. Children see the beauty of nature and respond . . . they hear the music of life and sing . . . they are aware of the beauty all around them. Somewhere in our growing up, we manage to lose most of this rapture and childlike delight in living.

I have three rules from St. Ignatius which have helped me discover the abundant life. They also can help you live while your heart is pumping blood.

I *came from God.* Whether or not you believe in a divine intelligence in the orthodox manner or just feel that Someone is out there somewhere, you must be aware that this universe is a planned composite of order and beauty. Man must have come from an Intelligent Being. Because I believe this I can make sense of my life. I need a Point of Reference that is absolute and perfect, since I am finite and imperfect. I need Someone to worship who is just and honest, forgiving and merciful. I find this in God. I believe I came from him with some of the attributes which he possesses; this enables me to forgive and be honest and seek justice and mercy for my fellows.

I *belong to God.* His life flows through me and around me. I can see it in each individual I meet. All life is precious and of great worth. This affects my judgment and every decision with which I am faced. It can bring purpose out of chaos. It assures me that I am not alone.

I *return to God.* At death I simply return from where I came. Eternity is the home of the heart. I know death will be beautiful for it must transcend the misery and pain which every human endures. Yet I do not have to wait for death to feel this comradeship with eternity, for eternity is now. Today is a part of eternity. Death removes the restrictions which bind, and I am confident that although we fail to understand it, life continues beyond the grave in much the same manner as it does here except that new dimensions are added. I have no fear of death, because I see it as an extension of life.

"Man is that he might have joy." How tragic if you live beneath your potential! Celebrate your existence by recognizing the "possibilities hidden in the edges of life, even while [you] are aware of all the evil." Celebrating is growing and becoming as long as you live. There is one element which can bring you to life—caring. Care for yourself and every other human being. Don't be ashamed of your feelings for others; be ashamed only if you feel little for them. Devotion is more than emotion or instant love. The sharing of the pain and agony of life means being willing to be born anew—even in travail. You tune in to life as you experience life processes in a mood of celebration.

Celebrating is capturing the magic of life and throwing it away to everyone you meet. It's the joy of being you, here and now. It's discovering the spirit of play as well as the spirit of prayer. It is enjoying the ordinary things that go into ordinary lives on ordinary days. It's seeing every day in an extraordinary way, regardless of what comes.

Every day is a happy birthday. Rejoice . . . you're alive! Celebrate your existence!

The whole world is a theater of life, an inexhaustible universe for man to ex-

plore, invent, and test. . . . There is always more to understand and to be. . . . We keep working at it, and therefore stay alive.

—*Ross Snyder*

EPILOGUE

This is a day in which the foundations of our world have been shaken. It is a time when many have been pulled under by the hopelessness which seemingly exists in our fragmented society. Yet I must affirm my confidence and assurance. I intend to keep right on celebrating my existence as I challenge life on every front. I cannot do it alone. I need all of you. So does the world. We need to plunge into the depths of the mystery which is life and together rediscover a cause for celebration.

I see a new day dawning, and I desire to be a part of that newness. Step through a rainbow, my friend, into the glory which is humanity's inheritance. Then shout with me . . .

> I see it coming, Lord!
> Within my heart
> I feel the glory of that day,
> When men shall walk as brothers
> In the Way.
>
> I hear a new sound, Lord.
> And I rejoice
> To sense the splendor of earth's dawn

As meaning like a leaping fire
Catches on.

Within my being, Lord,
There surges forth
Assurance of thy timeless plan.
Behold! The beauty of thy love
Begins in man!

And this is only the beginning. Hopelessness
shall fade in tomorrow's fulfillment. And you'll be
there! See you, friend!

Lucille

SUGGESTED READING

Prayer Can Change Your Life, by Dr. William Parker, Prentice-Hall, Inc.

On Becoming Human, by Ross Snyder, Abingdon Press

Are You Running with Me, Jesus? by Malcolm Boyd

The Whole World Is Watching, by Mark Gerzon, Paperback Library, N. Y.

The Art of Loving, by Erich Fromm, World Perspective Series

The Healing of Persons, by Paul Tournier, Harper and Row

You Are Not the Target, by Laura Huxley, Farrar, Straus and Company, N. Y.

The Stress of Life, by Hans Selye, M.D., McGraw-Hill

The Doctor and the Soul, by Viktor E. Frankl, M.D., a Bantam Book

Search for Meaning, by Viktor E. Frankl, M.D.

Dialogue with Myself, by Martin C. D'Arcy, S.J., The Credo Series—Pocket Books, Inc.

Peace of Mind, by Joshua Loth Liebman, Simon and Schuster, N. Y.